OUR SOLEMN OATH

A CALL TO WAKE UP

Kieran T Davis

DEDICATION

For the ones who feel overlooked, underestimated, and forgotten.

For the curse-breakers, the cycle-enders, the dreamers.
May God's will be done.

CONTENTS

AUTHOR'S NOTE / PREFACE

Independent thinking is not your enemy—it only *seems* that way at first. By the end of this book, I hope it becomes your ally. Don't read these pages as absolute fact; read them as perspective. In truth, most of what we speak, write, and consume—articles, books, conversations—is analysis, perspective, and hypothesis. Even "facts" can look different depending on where you stand, like looking at the number 6 from opposite sides.

Be slow to judge and quick to understand. The human experience is complex, and I pray this work helps as many people as possible. This book is not complete, and it is not perfect—because my understanding of the world is not complete. Perhaps in ten years, I'll have more to offer. But if you're just beginning this journey— or haven't pondered these ideas for long—much of what you read here may feel profound.

I wrestled with God before writing this. It took a year before I could truly begin. Yet here I am, tying a bow on a finished work—grateful, humbled, and at peace.

If you are not a believer in God or in Christ, I invite you to read with a soft heart and an open mind. We don't have to agree on everything to learn something meaningful from one another.

THE OATH

This book is not just something to read, it's something to live. If you're holding this, it's because you're being called to something deeper. Not louder, flashier, or deeper.

You're tired of drifting, tired of feeling like something's missing, and deep down, you know... It's time to wake up.

This isn't about hype or motivation. It's about mastery.
Self. Spirit. Purpose.
This is for the ones who weren't handed a blueprint.
The ones who had to learn everything the hard way.
The ones who feel the weight of legacy and refuse to pass down pain.
If that's you, then this book was written for you.

And this is your Oath:
To grow on purpose.
To live with purpose.
And never surrender your purpose.
What you do next is up to you.
But once you turn this page, you're in it now.
No turning back.

DISCLAIMER

This book is not for the faint of heart. It will challenge you to reflect, confront uncomfortable truths, and take full responsibility for your life. If you are unwilling to self-reflect, this message may not resonate with you, and that's okay.

But if you are ready to break cycles, stop drifting, and step boldly into your purpose, this is your call to action.

MY SOLEMN OATH

I, _____, fully commit to breaking the cycles that have held me back.

I pledge to:

- Pursue my God-given purpose with courage and consistency.
- Build a life rooted in discipline, faith, and integrity.
- Reject drifting, excuses, and anything that keeps me stagnant.
- Lead myself and those connected to me toward growth and freedom.

This is not just a promise, it's a declaration, because today, I choose to rise, to stand firm, and to live differently.

Signature: _____

Date: _____

Wake Up

Do You Know Who You Are?

I would argue that most people don't fully understand who they are. Sure, they know what makes them laugh, and they know what makes them mad, but ask them about their **purpose**, and you'll probably get blank stares.

Try it, ask someone close to you, "Why do you exist?" They'll likely get confused.

Ask again, and I promise you, 9 out of 10 times, you'll hear something like: *"To provide for my kids."*

If they have children, that's the default response, but here's the thing: that's a **responsibility**, not a purpose. It's part of their role as a mother or father, but it's not the reason they exist.

I would go even further and argue: if you don't understand your purpose in life, you can't possibly have a good sense of self.

Think about it. Let's say you own a TV but have no idea what it's for. Could we say you understand what a TV is?

What about a can opener, a lawn mower, or a bottle opener?

We know the purpose of so many things, yet when it comes to the most important question of all, *"Why do you exist?"*, so many are completely unaware.

Your life truly begins the day you come to that realization. The day you **wake up**.

The World Has Been Molding You

Throughout your life, the world has been shaping you to fit its image, an image that serves other people's egos.

Your parents mold you into someone they can brag about. So do your grandparents, aunts, uncles, and siblings. They all have a version of who they think you should be, and they try to turn you into that person.

Then you go off to school, and your teachers continue the molding process. So do your peers. And on and on it goes.

Eventually, we begin to **seek approval** just to feel valid. We look for signals, nods, affirmations, anything that says, *"Yes, you're doing it right."*

Sometimes I wonder: what if I had grown up in another country, another town, another household? What if I had a different set of friends? What if I had married someone else? How different would I be?

We are products of our environments. So how can anyone say they truly know who they are if the character they're playing was shaped entirely by the people and places around them?

So many of us are actors, performing a role that was handed to us at birth.
We had little say in shaping the character we now live as.
And truthfully, we're afraid to wake up, because once we do, nothing around us will make sense anymore.

To wake up would mean facing the fact that every day we've been playing a part in someone else's script.
But most people would rather **live a lie and feel accepted** than question their reality.

There is a way out of this.

But first, the current version of you must **die**.

Kill the Illusion, Not Yourself

I'm speaking **figuratively**, of course. Don't kill yourself.

First of all, this version of you was never your true self anyway.
And second, the moment you wake up, you begin to **develop your true self.**

You must understand your purpose and identify your unique gifts. Those two things become your compass as you begin crafting who you're truly supposed to be.

Now, at this point, anyone afraid of change, anyone stubborn or closed-minded, they've probably stopped reading already.

If you're still here, I'm going to assume one of three things:

1. You're intrigued.
2. You agree.
3. Or you're still trying to figure out how this applies to your life.

Either way, let me make it plain.

Drifting Through Life

If you don't know your purpose in life, **you are not truly living**. You're drifting, wandering with no real direction. And chances are, everyone around you is doing the same.

Like attracts like.
So those who know their purpose tend to move with others who know theirs.
You can feel it in their energy. They speak differently. Move differently. Think differently.

There's an intentionality behind their actions and their words.

The term "drifters" was coined by Napoleon Hill in his book *Outwitting the Devil.*
It refers to people who are essentially under a spell, going through life on autopilot, doing the devil's work without even realizing it.

What does that look like?

Let's say your mom or your spouse sends you to the store for milk.

On the way, you get distracted. You get home, and you've got a loaf of bread instead.

You forgot the mission.

That's how many people are living. They were sent here with a purpose. But they've gotten distracted, lost track of their mission, and they don't even realize it.

A Life Lived for Distractions

Let me give you a personal example.

When I was a kid, I used to play *Grand Theft Auto: San Andreas*. And yeah, I had no business playing that game at my age, but it is what it is. Childhood had its moments.

In the game, there was a full storyline, a structured mission path you could follow, like in most video games. But *San Andreas* had all these other things you could do: ride bikes, start fights, customize your character, and explore random places.

And guess what?
Most people never beat the game.

They got so caught up in the distractions, they forgot the storyline even existed.

That's exactly what we're doing in real life.

We're indulging in all the distractions. We're prioritizing the temporary. We're choosing entertainment over enlightenment. And we've completely abandoned the storyline, our *purpose*.

Most people would rather stay asleep.
But if you want to get the most out of your life, then make an oath to complete this book.

Because I'm going to share everything I know to help you stop drifting, to help you **wake up**, and to help you live as your true self, not the version of you that was scripted by others.

You can't live your truth until you stop living their lie.

Our Father & Design

Get Present

Focus on your breath, be very present right now.

Feel your heartbeat.
Wiggle your fingers.
Take in your surroundings.

Everything in this world is connected, and everyone in this world is connected.
The trees exist for a reason.
The birds in the sky, the animals in the fields, the fish in the sea, even the sponges filtering the ocean floor, are all living on purpose.

But somewhere along the way, many men and women disconnect from this, because they lose sight of this sense of belonging.

You Exist Because You're Needed

I firmly believe that every person exists because the world needs them. God called them into existence for a reason, and that you were born into this exact moment, in time and on purpose, not by accident.

The challenge for many is that they feel **insignificant.** But I would argue that feeling only exists when you're disconnected from the truth.

Look at nature. Even the spiders, creatures most people fear, serve their purpose.

So why would you think you're the one exception?

You're Not Too Small, And You're Not Too Big

I hold a very specific perspective:

I'm not so insignificant that only bad things can happen to me, but I'm also not so significant that only good things can happen to me.

I don't see myself as better than anyone, but I'm also fully aware that no one is better than me.

It's like that old saying: *"Don't judge a fish by its ability to fly."*

We all have different gifts and unique talents, special, intentional, and given by God for our appointed roles in this world.

Humility and Confidence Can Coexist

I have the **humility** to know that I'm not the center of the universe; God is.

But I also have the **confidence** to know that God made me specifically for His plan, His purpose, and His will.

And guess what?

That same truth applies to **you**.

This Is Not About Religion

I want to be clear: I'm not here to preach religion, and I'm also not here to convince you that God exists. If you look around, really observe the intricacies and complexity of this world, I believe any intelligent person can come to that conclusion on their own.

So I'll assume you're intelligent enough to skip past that debate.

Instead, I want to talk about what that understanding means for your life.

Your Role in the Bigger Picture

You play a very important role in this thing called life, but most of us tend to hyper-focus on ourselves, our families, and our close friends.

That's natural.

But if **everything is connected**, shouldn't I care about your child the way I care about my own?

Now, I might not love them the same, I might not know their names, but if we're truly all connected, if we all matter, then I should still move through life with your child in mind when I'm building my future.

Because if my only consideration is *me* and *mine*, how can I ever make a real impact on the world?

Ego Must Die Before Purpose Can Live

I think about leaders who have national holidays named after them, Dr. King, Abraham Lincoln, and, sadly, Christopher Columbus. Each of them (in different ways) had to experience the *death of their ego* for the sake of something bigger than themselves.

For a man or woman to truly be led by God, the ego must die. God has no use for your ego, your pride, or your expectations. Those are the very things the *enemy* uses to distract and destroy you.

What I Mean by "The Enemy"

When I say *"the enemy,"* here's what I mean:

Someone who seeks to *kill, steal, and destroy.*
Someone who cheers for your downfall.
Someone who stands in direct opposition to Our Father.

And unlike robots, we were given *free will*. That's part of the power of being human. You can choose obedience. You can choose alignment. And when you do, joy, peace, abundance, and success follow, not by chance, but as *promises from God.*

The enemy can't take those promises from you, but what the enemy can do, and does masterfully, is **trick you.**

He convinces you to choose fear instead of faith, pride instead of surrender, and lust instead of love. Greed, gluttony, ego, all of it before God, and when you follow those impulses, you **forfeit** what's rightfully yours.

You don't lose your blessings because they were taken; you lose them because you gave them away, and in so doing, you settle for a life of disappointment, confusion, and quiet misery when joy and abundance were always on the table.

P.S.: I serve Jesus Christ, the only true way to the Father, and invite you to explore a relationship with him individually.

God doesn't need your perfection. He needs your surrender.

CHAPTER

3

Built for a Reason

You Beat the Odds

1 in 400 trillion.

Those are the odds of being born. The first time I heard that, I thought it was insane.

Just consider what had to happen for you to exist: The complications that can happen during pregnancy...
The chances of successful conception...
Even the odds of your mother and father being attracted to each other in the first place.

Now copy and paste that process back to the **very first man and woman**, and you'll begin to see how many things had to align for you to be here. That realization always reminds me that I'm not here by accident and I exist because of **favor, purpose, and intentionality.**

Do You Know Why You're Here?

Do you know your purpose? Why are you here?
Why did God bring you into this world?

In my experience, the true meaning of life is developing the **quality of that picture**, the picture of your purpose. The person who has the **clearest vision** of why they're here is not only the most successful... They're also the most joyful, and if anyone in this life should be envied, it would be them.

Allow me to give you a map, something to help you stop drifting and start developing that picture. I've worked on mine for years, and I'm still sharpening it, because purpose isn't a destination; it's an **interstate**, a long road filled with peace, joy, and fulfillment that you ride out until the very end.

What Is Your Gift?

Let's start with a big question: *What is your gift?*

I'll be honest, I hate this question, not because it's unimportant, but because it's **so loaded.** It could be its own chapter, even its own book.

We all have many gifts, some are easy to identify because they're common or praised, others are rare, hidden, or unrecognizable until you try enough new things and discover: *Hey... I'm actually good at this.*

So don't rush it. This path is an **interstate**, remember, not a finish line, and if you're lucky, you'll keep discovering new gifts as life unfolds.

Let's simplify:
Traditionally, a "gift" is seen as a spiritual thing, while a "talent" is more secular.

But I'll just use the word **gift**, because I believe every good thing we're given comes from God, no matter how it shows up.

So ask yourself this:

> *What's something I do better than most people... with the least amount of effort?*

Look Beneath the Surface

I like to get to the **root** of things.

Here's why:
Someone might say, *"I'm a gifted researcher."*
But the real gift might be **curiosity**.

We often mistake the **expression** of the gift for the gift itself.

Another example:
A person may say their gift is public speaking; that's what they've been praised for, but I'd argue the real gift is **communication**, or maybe even **connection**. The ability to move people with words, to make someone feel something, that can't be taught.

The same goes for entrepreneurs. Someone says, *"I'm good at building businesses."*
But what fuels that? It could be **vision**, the ability to see something before it exists. To hold an idea in your mind and bring it to life. That's the root; everything else is just the fruit that grows from it.

Root First. Fruit Later.

You might be the one your friends go to for advice, the one who always knows what to say. That's not just a personality trait. That's **empathy**.

You feel what others feel, and you're not afraid to sit in it with them; that's not just a gift, it's spiritual.

We spend so much time praising the **fruit**: what people do, achieve, or display, but fruit comes and goes with the seasons.

The **root** is what sustains life. If you want a life that can weather storms, you've got to figure out your roots. When you live from that place, your true gift, whatever life cuts down will grow again.

That's the power of being **rooted** in purpose, not **performance**.

Here's the secret most people miss:
The fruit was never the goal. The root was.
Because the root is where your identity lives.

A Real-World Example: Steph Curry

Take basketball. Anyone can learn to play, but you could train for 100 years and still never shoot like Stephen Curry. People say he's a "gifted shooter", and they're not wrong.

But I'd argue his **shooting ability** is just the **branch**. His **championships and records**? That's fruit. The **real gift** is his **ability to hyper-focus**.

There's even a video online of Steph hitting a hole-in-one while golfing.

If he had focused on golf instead of basketball, he might've been one of the greats there, too. That's what it feels like to operate in your gift. Like a superpower.

Gifts, Strengths, and Fruit

Your gift comes from God to assist you with your **purpose** here on Earth. Once you identify your gift(s), your next job is to develop **strengths** around them. If your gift is the **root**, then your strengths are the **branches**.

And the **fruit**? That's what gets produced: your possessions, your experiences, your impact.

For some, fruit might look like land, cars, and assets, while for others, it's moments, memories, and legacy. And while I could write a whole book on this, let's get back to the main road: **purpose.**

The Adventure You're Built For

Think of your life like an **adventure**, a real quest. Now imagine this:
You've just been **called** to something greater.
A journey. A mission.
You don't have all the details yet, but deep down, you know...
You were built for it.

That's your **purpose.** The call to step into something meaningful. The path you were designed to walk.

You Were Equipped from the Start

But no adventurer leaves home empty-handed. You've been **equipped** with something. A tool, weapon, something sacred. Something only you carry.

That's your **gift.**

It's not decoration, it's your advantage in the battle ahead. Some are gifted with vision, others with strategy, empathy, discipline, or creativity, so whatever yours is, it's there for a reason, and it was given to you **before** the battle even began.

Find the Fire Behind the Fight

Every journey has a reason behind it; that reason is your **passion.**

It's the fire that burns in you, injustice you can't ignore, vision you can't shake, problem you're here to solve, future you're determined to build, and passion fuels your purpose.

It gives your gift **direction;** without it, you're just swinging your sword in the dark.

Let's Break It Down

Let me simplify it like this:

- **Purpose** is the call to adventure.

- **A gift** is the weapon you carry on the journey.

  _____

  _____

  _____

- **Passion** is the reason you picked up the sword in the first place.

  _____

  _____

  _____

You Were Built to Win

Like any real adventure, you won't always know what's coming next, but if you honor your gift, follow your purpose, and stay connected to your passion, you won't just survive the journey... **You'll win.**

Your gift is not for applause, it's for impact.

CHAPTER

Refinement

The Breaking Point

I've spent the last 10+ years of my life focused on personal and professional development. I didn't even know the self-help world existed until I was 19. A kid growing up in poverty…homeless in middle school and high school… I used to think I was cursed.

At 19, I moved away from home and began walking a dark path of **drugs, sex, and alcohol.** Yes, I was addicted to weed, to alcohol, and to chasing women.

Those were my bandages, and that's how I numbed my pain. I was living fast, trying to find ways to make money, and it led to my getting put on probation. I was lost, and worse, I had forsaken myself, but that pain brought me closer to God, and Christ made sure I came across a quote by Maria Robinson:

> *"No one can go back and make a new beginning, but anyone can start today and make a new ending."*

That was the first time in my life that I stopped feeling like a victim. I started to feel *empowered*, in control, for once, I believed I could become a different version of myself, the **truest, most authentic** version of me.

You Weren't Born This Way

When we're young, we're just sponges, soaking in everything around us and calling it "normal."

The way we talk.
How we walk.
What we think is cool.
All of it is influenced by our surroundings.

This is why the wealthy want their kids in certain schools and out of certain neighborhoods. **Influence is constant.** And unless we filter what we allow into our space, it will shape us by default.

Some of us, like me, were surrounded by negative influence simply because of **proximity.**

In truth, most people never decide who they are; they become a character molded by their environment. You didn't **choose** to be the person you are right now. And that's why so many people carry insecurities and feel out of place.

To find who you're supposed to be, you've got to go inward. You've got to look at your heart, get in touch with your soul, and **refine** the version of you that the world didn't create.

The Mind Must Be Rewired

I didn't realize how broken my thinking was until I got exposed to *new thinking*, new perspectives, and new paradigms.

So I went on a mission to **reprogram my mind.**

I read book after book, and took pride in it, not just for personal growth, but because I was a Black man fighting a stereotype.

Think about it, people spend their entire lives gathering wisdom and knowledge... and then pour it into a book for the next willing soul to receive.

Books were my first mentors, first coaches, and I was thirsty, thirsty to grow, thirsty to run from the version of myself I no longer wanted to be.

Knowledge Isn't Power, Application Is

Over time, I hit a wall, even though I was learning so much... something felt off.

I realized: **knowledge isn't power. Applied knowledge is power.**

All the information in the world means nothing if you don't know how or where to apply it. Studying engineering is meaningless if I have no desire to be an engineer. We don't know what we don't know. And without direction, even a library can become a distraction.

So I had to **focus.**
What did I want?

I wanted to break **generational curses.**
I wanted **financial freedom.**

So I stopped reading everything and started reading only about *that.*

What Separates the Wealthy from the Poor?

Why do less than 10% of people earn six figures?
Why do fewer than 1% become millionaires?

What do they know that our communities don't?

Once I started studying the **patterns,** it all became clear:

Everything is different.
The conversations. The mindsets. The priorities.
The way they dress, speak, view money, and value time. The wealthy and the poor live in opposite worlds; we do all the same things, just in **opposite ways.**

The Reason for Refinement

Before I go any deeper, let me say this:

Personal development is useless if done for the wrong reason.
Self-help, business books, mentorship, fitness, therapy, it all means nothing if you don't understand your **why.**

That's why this chapter comes after purpose, gifts, and passion, because **refinement only matters when you know what you're refining for.**

I'm not developing myself just for the hell of it.

I'm refining myself because I know my **mission.**
I know what I want, and I know I have to become a sharper, more aligned version of myself to reach it.

Time only moves forward. So if you're not growing, you're falling behind.

Growth or Regression, There's No In-Between

We're like plants, constantly in motion, you're either growing, or you're dying, and if you're staying the same while time keeps moving forward, then you're falling behind. Not just behind your peers or society, but behind the **best version of you.**

And if you're regressing? That's even worse.

I have very little sympathy for choosing comfort over growth. My deepest desire is to experience **everything God created**, to travel, taste, explore, laugh, love, and live fully.

And yes, that takes money. But even more, it takes becoming someone worthy of that experience.

The Cost of Stagnation

I don't want to live as the version of me that was **addicted,** insecure, and mediocre. Those traits can't coexist with a life of abundance and freedom.

Sure, you can visit Italy.
But did you shop in Milan?
Did you sit in the front row at fashion week?
Did you do it as your **best self?**

I want to make decisions based on *desire*, not *lack*.
Not *"I can't."*
Not *"I wish."*
Every day I wake up in the reality I don't want, it pisses me off.

The Three Timelines of Life

There are three timelines in life:

1. The one you're currently on.

2. The one where you're growing with intention.

3. And the one where you're doing nothing.

_____

_____

_____

Each version of you is surrounded by different people, in different places, with different habits, health, finances, and outcomes. On one of those timelines, you might be in jail or worse, dead.

We owe it to ourselves, our families, and to **God to grow** with intention. It's how we show **gratitude** for the life we were given.

You Will Never Be Perfect, And That's the Point

Let me be clear: you'll never be perfect.

That's not the goal.

You're a human being. You're here to **feel, to fail, to struggle, to overcome,** and that's the **point** of this experience.

That's why we admire people who've faced real hardship and still chose to evolve.

Can You Handle the Blessing?

Growing up, I always heard:

> _"God won't give you more than you can handle."_

But here's what I realized: Some people aren't blessed yet because the blessing is **too heavy** for them.

If \$100K magically dropped into your account today, you'd probably act out. You'd lose your mind over money that isn't even life-changing. You simply aren't ready for your dreams to come true.

The blessing is **waiting for you,** not the other way around.

Your Life Depends on Your Development

Let me say this with love:

If you don't live your purpose... If you don't pursue your potential... If you don't refine yourself into the version of you that God created...Your life will feel **empty.**

And you will die full of **what-ifs** and *"if onlys."*

Can God trust you with this journey?

Will you show up every day with **intentionality?**

Will you cut off the people and habits that hold you back?

We all start life at **Level 1.**

But the only way to level up is through **knowledge, action, and alignment** with purpose.

You don't need more time; you just need to **get out of your way.**

Refine yourself, because God's plan is already laid out.

All he's waiting on... Is **You**.

You can't become your future self by staying loyal to your past.

CHAPTER

5

Mind & Body

Mental Health Is Foundational

Over the years, I've learned that our **mental health is essential to our success.** There are a few practices that create a **compound effect,** and everyone should take full advantage of them.

The first one? ***Working out.***

Exercise is one of the most powerful and underused antidepressants. When my last business failed, I felt ashamed, ashamed because I knew how many people assumed I was winning.

My brand was growing. I was riding high, but when that crumbled, so did my mental health. God helped pull me through that season, and one of the tools he gave me was the gym.

I worked out at least five days a week. I was focused, intentional. Every rep helped take my mind off the chaos. I became obsessed with **getting stronger**, physically and mentally.

And over time, I realized:
What I was learning in the gym could be transferred to other areas of my life.

The Discipline of Delay

Most people struggle because they crave **instant gratification.** Working out deprives us of that. It forces us to focus on **long-term consistency** over short-term comfort, but I've never once finished a workout and regretted showing up.

That's the beauty of it.

Working out is dedicating time **today** for results **six months from now.** We know that one workout won't transform us, but if we stay consistent, the results will come. That same logic applies to every area of life, our **finances**, our **relationships**, and our **mindsets.**

Fitness as a Framework

Working out teaches you structure:

- You plan your workouts.

  _____

  _____

  _____

- You track your progress.

  _____

  _____

  _____

- You count your reps and weight.

  _____

  _____

  _____

- You learn discipline.

  _____

  _____

  _____

- You start being mindful of what you eat.

  _____

  _____

  _____

You even start learning about health, things like macros, hydration, and sleep cycles. It's all connected. If more people took fitness seriously, they would improve in almost **every other area** of their lives.

That's why I tell anyone going through a dark time: **Stay in the gym,** and even when things are going well, **keep going.**

If you're consistent with the things that helped you survive the hard times, you'll be better prepared when life throws the next punch.

Journaling for Clarity

Another tool I've come to value is **journaling.** There are so many thoughts and emotions we carry every day, things we struggle to articulate or express, sometimes it's because the people around us won't understand, other times, it's because *we* haven't processed it yet.

Journaling gives you a space to **dump the mental weight.**

It keeps you from being overwhelmed.
It allows you to show up as your best self, even when your mind feels messy.

It doesn't have to be perfect; it just has to be **real.**

Keep Feeding Your Mind

If there's one thing I believe in deeply, it's this:
Always stay a student. Always keep learning.

As a Black man, I take it personally that the statistics on reading in our community are so low.

When I was in college, I made it a goal to read at least 12 books a year. Over time, that number grew as my hunger for growth grew. I mainly read self-help, business, psychology, and anything that I could immediately apply to my life. And every time, I'd close the book and think:

"Wow, I wish I had read this sooner."

There's something sacred about the idea that men and women live full lives, gather wisdom through pain and trial, and then take the time to write a book so someone like me doesn't have to suffer the same way.

You Don't Know What You Don't Know

There are so many things I've learned about myself, about life, that I **never would've found on my own.** I wouldn't have even known what to look for, but a book put it in front of me.

That's why I challenge you: **Have a thirst for knowledge.**

Don't stay the same, and don't wait for life to force growth through painful lessons; educate yourself before the world has to do it the hard way.

Most people stop learning after high school, but life keeps teaching, with or without your permission.

And for those of us who didn't grow up in homes where we were nurtured and developed?

We have to go our own way.
We have to develop **ourselves.**

Growth Shouldn't Cost Connection

Now, don't get me wrong, I'm not saying that growth is more important than enjoyment or relationships, but growth is necessary.

Still, I never want you to be so locked in that you look up and find yourself completely alone. **Human connection matters.**

If you have friends you can read books with, hit the gym with, and sharpen each other mentally and spiritually, **you are blessed.**

Value those people.

But if you don't? Don't force it, don't try to drag your friends into your growth journey. Do it for yourself, and when the time is right, your tribe will find you.

When Nothing Else Is Working

Lastly, I want to speak to the person who feels stuck.

Maybe life isn't working out the way you expected. You feel like there's no progress, no peace. Just the same mistakes on repeat.

Let me leave you with this:

Even when everything else feels like it's falling apart… You can always find success in these three things:

- **Working out**

  _____

  _____

  _____

- **Reading books**

  _____

  _____

  _____

- **Journaling for mental clarity**

  _____

  _____

  _____

These are your anchors; they are simple, foundational practices that will always give more than they take.

And if you stay grounded in them? You'll make it through.

Growth doesn't always look like success. Sometimes it looks like showing up.

Produce & Prosper

The Two Types of Economic Mindsets

There are two kinds of people in this world, economically: **producers and consumers**. These groups fundamentally think differently.

Now, everyone spends money, buys things, and consumes. And honestly, by default, everyone is an entrepreneur in some way. However, not everyone is a producer in the sense of offering their own product and/or service to the market.

What often happens is we sell our services to companies, we fill out a W-2, and accept an hourly wage or salary in exchange for our time. The issue with this is that you're limited to what someone else believes your services are worth. If you work at Starbucks, they've already created a job description for you, defining the scope of the role you're being hired to fulfill.

Once you realize that your value shouldn't be limited to what someone else is willing to pay you, you start to think like a **producer.**

I'm not telling people not to work jobs; jobs are great, and there are ways to climb that ladder, too.

I'm simply saying: even if you are working a job, still produce something you can offer to the market.

Not everyone has to build a multi-million-dollar business. But everyone can make an extra $10,000 to $20,000 per year just by becoming a producer. And let's be honest, who couldn't use an extra $10–20K to help with bills or elevate their lifestyle?

Time Is Money, But It's Also Limited

Once you understand that you cannot exchange time for money forever, you're on the right path. As we get older, our time becomes more limited, making it more valuable. That's basic economics: **supply and demand.**

At 16, you might be fine taking a minimum-wage job. But at 30? That hits different. Not only is your time more valuable, but you've got responsibilities now. On top of that, you've gained skills that set you apart from others in the job market.

Everything starts to come together for your betterment, but only if you're intentional.

I've worked in the business sector for most of my professional life, in management, banking, and business advising. All of those experiences are now sharpening me, helping me become more well-rounded and a greater asset to any company willing to pay what I'm truly worth.

That also applies to those who go the route of college degrees or certifications. But whether you climb the ladder upward or laterally, eventually you'll hit a wall. No one is going to put you in a position to out-earn them or pay you what you're truly worth. When it comes to climbing the ladder, most people are grossly underpaid, while producers at the highest level are paid exactly for their skill set, knowledge, and sacrifices.

What stops most people is fear, in some form. But fear can be overcome by simplifying your journey, just take one step forward each day.

Start With What You Already Know

Now, you might be thinking:

> *"Well, what can I do to become a producer? How can I make extra money while working my day job and potentially build something I can retire early from?"*

Earlier, we talked about purpose, gifts, and passions. Reflect on that.

- What's something you do better than most people, with the least amount of effort?

- What's something you're passionate about, something you could talk about for hours, for free?

_____

_____

_____

When you start asking those questions, you're heating up.

Solve a Problem, Then Sell the Solution

Now, figure out how you can take that skill set and passion and **solve problems** for other people.

Maybe you're into fitness and weight loss, and others struggle with what to buy when trying to eat healthy. You could create digital products or courses that teach people what to buy, and just as importantly, what not to buy.

That kind of product is crucial when it comes to escaping the time-for-money trap. These are products you create once, but can sell over and over again.

You could also offer to go grocery shopping with clients or set up weekly accountability calls. Yes, that brings you back to trading time for money, but that's okay if you price it right.

Price to Smile, Not to Settle

Here's how you handle that: **price the offer in a way that makes you smile.**

If someone gave me $5,000, I'd feel good spending eight weeks working closely with them. I'd feel good stepping away from my family and hobbies to pour into them and ensure they get results. And if they're serious about the outcome I'm offering, they'll be happy to pay for the transformation.

Here's the irony: most people are afraid to sell or to ask for what they're worth, yet no one's uncomfortable spending money.

We've got to make that make sense.

Think about how many things you've dropped money on just because you wanted them: Shoes, jewelry, hairstyles, haircuts, vacations. Oh, and those overpriced drinks at bars and restaurants, when you could buy the whole bottle for the same price?

We can't keep making excuses when it comes to doing what's best for ourselves and our families.

Our time is far too valuable to give it away cheaply, especially if we're not investing time into the very things that will help us buy our time back.

Your Time, Your Terms

So let me ask you this: how many $5,000 offers would you need to sell each month to take care of your family?

For most Americans, maybe just one or two. Now imagine all the free time you'd have, not only to be present with your family and friends, but also to invest in yourself, your hobbies, and your peace of mind.

Wealth Requires a New Operating System

Building wealth requires a different mindset than the one that got you here. The way you currently think has you exactly where you are in life. If you want different results, you've got to move differently. If you don't change, but still expect new results, well, that's insanity.

You can snap out of that. You can break the cycle of being the same version of yourself every year.

And look, I'm not here to waste your time. I don't believe in fluff. I'm giving it to you straight.
It doesn't matter what your idea is, as long as there's a market for it, you need to be selling.

Not just selling, but thinking about how to build your offer in a way that lets you get paid repeatedly without needing to physically do anything after the first sale. **That's where freedom lives.**

Besides the value you will get from this book, you know what else I'm thinking about?

Why wouldn't I write this book?

CHAPTER

Temptation

The Danger of Losing It All

This chapter is extremely important because all your hard work, focus, and sacrifice can get washed away by one thing.

There are many temptations that men and women will face in life. Most of them are distractions meant to pull you away from your purpose, goals, and overall development. What makes them so difficult is that these distractions often feel natural to us.

When the Lie Sounds Like Love

So many men are taught in their youth to chase women, as if that's what life is about. I was caught by that lie, too. I felt driven by it. I even found purpose and meaning in it. Until one day, it all felt empty.

I realized I didn't just want attention, I wanted someone to grow with. Someone who truly knew me. Someone I could pour into and who could pour into me.

We're not meant to do life alone, but the process of finding a partner can be draining and difficult. To be honest, dating can be a massive distraction from your purpose. That's why I tell every man: ***know what you want in a woman.*** If you don't, you'll end up chasing looks, body, and sexual attraction, only to find out there's nothing deeper under the surface.

You repeat the cycle with multiple women, wasting your time and money, and in the end, only ruin your chances of finding a real-life partner. You may even have children with the wrong woman, and those mistakes are too expensive.

Be Realistic, Be Intentional

I challenge both men and women to define what they truly want in a partner. And be mindful that ***you'll be lucky to find 80% of that.*** The remaining 10–20% comes from growing together, through challenges, through patience, through learning.

Some lessons just won't be learned outside of relationships, because we're simply not motivated enough to care when we're alone. But love will force you to grow.

Women: if you choose the wrong man to lead you, he can push you to grow in the wrong direction. And the same goes for men. Understanding your purpose in life should always come first.

Why? ***Because you can't identify distractions if you don't even know where you're headed.***

Choosing the Right Person

Finding the right partner to do life with is one of the most important decisions you'll ever make. This is the person you'll spend the majority of your time with.

My wife and I have been together since we were 21 years old. It's not perfect, because we're human. But coexisting with someone is worth it when it's the right person.

Ask yourself:

- Do they bring peace into your life?

- Do they bring joy, love, comfort?

- Do they challenge you to grow in the right direction?

- Do they give you space and grace to fall and make mistakes?

- Is there respect for your individuality, and a mutual understanding that you are one?

_____

_____

_____

Marriage reveals a lot:

1. That you know what you want.

_____

_____

_____

2. That you can commit.

_____

_____

_____

3. That you believe in something larger than yourself.

_____

_____

_____

4. That you acknowledge God's plan for humans.

_____

_____

_____

5. That you've developed self-control over your fleshly desires.

_____

_____

_____

Be cautious of the company you keep. And be even more cautious of the person you choose to do life with. Choosing wrong can completely change the trajectory of your life.

The Real Battle

I say all this because I want you to be aware: ***our enemy will use your greatest desires to pull you off your purpose.***

Our desire for love can be manipulated into lust. We can become blinded and ignore the red flags. You must stay aware of your weaknesses, because temptation will come almost every day.

Some people allow their decisions to be led by their vices. But what desires do you have that could be used to exploit you?

- Love becomes lust.

_____

_____

_____

- Money becomes greed.

_____

_____

_____

- Comfort becomes complacency.

_____

_____

_____

There is a negative version of every positive, and the enemy knows how to use that.

Drifting into a Life You Never Chose

Don't lose yourself chasing what you desire. That's how drifting begins.

- You get stuck in a dead-end job because the money is just enough, while your goals collect dust.

_____

_____

_____

- You get stuck in a relationship that isn't fulfilling, but it's comfortable, so you stay.

_____

_____

_____

- You look up one day and realize none of it was what you truly wanted.

_____

_____

_____

Why? Because you never took the time to understand what you wanted. And let's be honest: *you can't lie to your heart.* It will always cry out for what it desires.

Sometimes we're just complaining. Sometimes we're ungrateful or unrealistic. But other times, we're certain, and yet still settling for less, or maybe we've been consumed by temptation, operating out of desire with no self-control or accountability.

Check Your Heart Daily

Continue to examine your heart, because there will be *many wars between your heart and your mind, your soul and your flesh.* That's the complexity of this life. We want to be certain. We want it to be simple. But no one wants to live a life that was built on a lie.

In the end, I pray you end up where you're destined to be. But know this: Christ is a gentleman. He will never force your hand. You have free will. And if you're not careful, you can end up living a life you were never meant for.

The wisdom is available.
The guidance is there, but you must choose to listen.

Don't let fear, doubt, worry, or anxiety rob you of what you know is meant for you.

Don't search for perfection, search for clarity. Search for alignment. And never forget:

> *"Desire without self-control is a trap. Don't let one moment of weakness cost you your future."*

Our Solemn Oath

A Message to the Generational Curse Breakers

Listen and hear me well.

I'm writing this for the generational curse breakers, for those like me who grew up with limited guidance, who dream of becoming the first in their family to go further. I know that one day I will no longer exist, and I don't want my efforts to be in vain.

I want to leave behind something real, something that helps others like me. I want to be for others what I needed most in my own life.

I'm not sharing this as someone who has it all figured out.

I don't.

I started in the wilderness, and I've learned, ***it's easier to start on the right path than to fight your way back to it.***

But I can share what I know. I can share what I'm committed to practicing, and I can speak to those of you who are ready to take this seriously, to pursue your God-given purpose with everything you have. To take the Oath: to succeed or die trying to fulfill God's will for your life.

But before you take that step, hear this:
This path is not comfortable.
It is mentally and emotionally exhausting.
But it is the only path worth walking.

Pick Your Poison

Growing up, I'd often hear people say, *"Life is hard, you just have to pick your poison."*

There are challenges when you live in lack.
There are challenges when you live in abundance.
But either way, you're going to face something challenging.

In our modern society, it's easy to forget that **simply staying alive is a challenge.** Avoiding car accidents, avoiding sickness, trying to keep your peace, that's all part of the daily battle. So I'm not here to scare you. I'm here to prepare you.

Because once you choose this path, the life you used to cling to will begin to reject you.

The Cost of Waking Up

Once you wake up, you'll begin to see your life in full clarity. And that can feel heavy. You might feel shame, embarrassment, or regret.

You'll notice the state of your own life, then you'll start seeing the lives of others around you. You'll want them to read this book. You'll try to get them to take the Oath, but they won't care.

And that will frustrate you, because you love them. You want them to win.

But let me be clear: *you can only control what you can control.*

Move forward without them, let your growth inspire them. If it doesn't, then nothing ever will.

You've chosen to grow, which means it's time to protect your energy. Guard your peace. Don't let negative influences derail your mindset.

Defining Negative Influence

What is a negative influence?

It's anything, or anyone, that goes against the life and lifestyle you're building. And that doesn't just mean people who verbally discourage you. It means anyone whose *lifestyle and direction* contradict your own.

The way a boxer trains is not how a basketball player trains. Not because one is wrong, but because each is preparing for a different mission.

Some people don't train at all because they're not headed anywhere, **and those are the ones you need to avoid.**

Humans are fruit. Ever heard the saying, *"One bad apple spoils the bunch"*?

Mold spreads. And if you want to thrive, you've got to stay away from spoiled fruit.

When the World Turns on You

Once you set boundaries, people will treat you differently.

They'll call you self-righteous.
They'll call you weird.
They'll isolate you.

But the truth is, they're just projecting their insecurities, because how dare you try to build a better life?

How dare you work on yourself and seek something more?

Your presence will irritate some people, your aura will feel different, your progress will offend them, and on a spiritual level, the warfare begins.

You were drifting through life, aligned with the enemy's purpose, not Christ's, but now that you've awakened, the enemy wants you back.

He'll use anything to pull you out of alignment: Friends, family, environments, habits.

Anyone still drifting, still overly drinking, still fornicating, ignoring their purpose, can be used as a tool against you.

That's why boundaries are everything.

You Might Feel Alone, But You're Not

This journey will get lonely at times.
But keep walking. Eventually, you'll find your tribe.

And while online support is great, in-person connections are vital.
Move to a new city if you have to.
Do what it takes to build the life you were designed for.

Boldness, Boundaries, and Being Disliked

Get comfortable being disliked.

Get comfortable being your authentic self.

To walk this out fully, you'll need boldness and assertiveness. I struggle with this too. I tend to overthink, and I don't want to act on assumptions. But I'm learning to lead with grace and still move with confidence.

Unshaken confidence comes with boldness, and boldness requires that you stop fearing what others think of you.

Not everyone will like you, but those cut from the same cloth will respect you.

The ones who won't?
They're usually insecure.
Still drifting.
Still filled with bitterness and self-hate.

That's not your problem.

Stay Grounded. Stay Growing.

Stay open-minded.
There's value in connecting with people from different places, different experiences, and different perspectives.

But never compromise your core.
Hold tight to your values. Your morals. Your principles.

Remain curious. Remain creative. Remain confident.

Because the best version of your life is waiting for you.

> **"You've taken the Oath, now walk it out. The world may not understand you, but God does."**

ACKNOWLEDGMENTS

First and foremost, I give honor to God, who has been my source, my strength, and my guide. Without His hand, this book would not exist.

To my wife, Leah, for her patience, love, and unwavering belief in me, even in the moments I doubted myself.

To my family, friends, and brothers who have walked with me through seasons of struggle and growth — thank you for sharpening me.

To my readers and supporters, who remind me daily why this message matters — your stories keep me going. This book is as much yours as it is mine.

ABOUT THE AUTHOR

Kieran T. Davis is an author, speaker, and business advisor who is passionate about helping men break cycles, rise into their God-given purpose, and build lasting legacies. His writing is raw, motivational, and grounded in faith — speaking directly to those who feel chosen but tested.

Kieran's mission extends beyond the page. He creates content across multiple platforms to reach people where they are, including three YouTube channels:

- **Kieran T Davis** — personal reflections on mindset, growth, and life lessons
- **Our Solemn Oath** — a channel dedicated to discipline, faith, masculine leadership, and legacy
- **1st Gen Founders** — practical and motivational content for aspiring entrepreneurs seeking to escape the "rat race" and build financial freedom

Through his words and his platforms, Kieran challenges others to reject drifting, face life with discipline, and live boldly in alignment with their calling.

Whether on the page, behind a camera, or in his community, he continues to push one message forward:

"Grow on purpose. Live with purpose. And never surrender your purpose."

Follow him on YouTube and Instagram: **@kierantdavis**

www.ingramcontent.com/pod-product-compliance
Lightning Source LLC
Chambersburg PA
CBHW020422150626
46554CB00014B/2353